The
She
Book

The
She
Book

Tanya Markul

Andrews McMeel
PUBLISHING®

Andrews McMeel Publishing
a division of Andrews McMeel Universal
1130 Walnut Street, Kansas City, Missouri 64106

www.andrewsmcmeel.com

19 20 21 22 23 BVG 10 9 8 7 6 5 4 3 2

ISBN: 978-1-5248-5106-4

Library of Congress Control Number: 2018966057

Editor: Katie Gould
Art Director: Diane Marsh
Production Editor: Amy Strassner
Production Manager: Carol Coe
Illustration by Tim Bjørn

ATTENTION: SCHOOLS AND BUSINESSES
Andrews McMeel books are available at quantity discounts with bulk purchase for educational, business, or sales promotional use. For information, please e-mail the Andrews McMeel Publishing Special Sales Department: specialsales@amuniversal.com.

You are already enthroned.
There is no putting down that crown.
Not a queen to a lover or community,
but a holier mystery, an angelic decree,
that will ever bend the knee,
to the fierce yet tender wand
of the awakening woman.

Tanya Markul

To the woman who told me,
"The dream, the darkness, and the moonlight
are also guides along your path."

For all the amazing women I've met
and the ones I haven't just yet . . .
I believe in your magic.
I bow to your risk.

This book is dedicated
to my beloved Christian and our sons,
the angelic Albert Leo and the kingly Arthur Holger.
I love you so very much.

about the book

Once a silent star in the sky, lost, alone, and unnoticed, she began to dream her life awake.

Sensitivity brought light to her dark side and vulnerability found words for what her heart felt but could not say.

Pain helped her remember the power within her storm, the wisdom in her breakdowns, and the healing visions hidden within her moonlit nightmares.

On her journey to shine from within her deepest ache, she blossomed from what felt like an insignificant twinkle to a blazing, awakening woman.

why 114

Because angels are close and everything's going to be all right, and the Universe is saying this is a blessed time of your life. Because the woman you are now marks a new beginning, and the woman you are becoming is calling you home and toward wholeness.

This is a place of remembering who you are and that you are made of wildness and filled with stars.

Come, sisters,
let us sit around the fire.

introduction

This is your time to return the call of grace. To not give up hope. To not look away. Because a hole exists in the world's broken heart. And it fits your exact shape. It doesn't take everyone. But those like you. Who hear the call and feel the ache. The souls who refuse cover in the wake of injustice. Of instability. Of silence. Who take shape like the towering cumulus of a fierce storm. They are seed planters of earth-bound mercy and warriors of a thunderous gold-covered love. They may not save it all, but quite a lot. They are angels born into shadow service. A knowing since their first breath. They speak the language of stars. Live in accordance with water and are guided by the wisdom of trees. They are rebels of compassion and freedom. They are torchbearers for peace. Their footprints lead to the other side of shadow.

Sister, look through the flames and around the circle. You were never alone in this feat. This is the courageous fire before the threshold of change. Woman, this is your time. And there is much to be danced. There is much to be undone.

opening ceremony

To the North within you,
may you express the wisdom of your true self.

To the West within you,
may you be reborn with every season.

To the South within you,
may you hear the counsel of your heart.

To the East within you,
may you be blessed with inner illumination.

To all Above that is within you,
may you be guided by angels and divinity.

To all Below that is within you,
may you discover the blessing of your shadow.

To the Spirit within you,
may you find your way home.

one

You see,
what they thought
was a phoenix
rising from its ashes,
was really
a woman.

two

For you, the torchbearer of pain,
you will be taught a different path
so that you can offer
the world
a new way.

three

Some days she wakes up
and her heart weighs 200 pounds
and her soul feels 10,000 years old.
And then she realizes
she's a journey made of stardust,
not just a human.

four

To learn
the language of love
is to unlearn
feeling homeless,
half-alive,
and less than whole.

five

She's in between worlds right now. A part of
her is leaving. But it's not like before. She's
holding space this time. Not sweating it, but
breathing beyond her skin. She's good. She's
even shape-shifting. The raven. The owl. She's
unafraid of the bird's-eye view, and unlike all
those other times, she isn't scared of the
unknown. She's present and neither timid nor
bold. It feels beautiful, like the song of a
blackbird, and frightening, like the rumble of
an avalanche.

six

If you lose yourself, it's not real.
If you abandon yourself, it's not worth it.
Not for love.
Not for attention.
Not for company.
Not for redemption.
Not for passing time.
Not for anything.
Not for anyone.

seven

Sometimes the scariest bridge to burn
is the one between you
and the person
you thought you were.

eight

Rejection
taught her to let go of what didn't want her.

Abandonment
showed her how to stand on her own two feet.

Betrayal
awoke her intuition.

Pain
broke her heart wide open.

Loneliness
gave her permission to befriend herself.

nine

When the shadows lay darkest,
remember you are made of stars.

When the shadows lay darkest,
whisper, "Challenge accepted."

When the shadows lay darkest,
wake up and feel.

ten

I wish I could remain calm and grounded. I wish I could change the pattern of incessantly reliving moments of being pushed down, hushed, and ignored. I wish I could set aside the fire-licking arrows I release when patience fails me. At times like these, I long for the taste of rain-soaked clouds.

eleven

The pain
that made you
the odd one out
is the story
that connects you
to a healing world.

twelve

When you feel defeated and deprived.
When you forget who you are.
When you have to break open.
Tell yourself what you need.
And how you want to be supported.

Stop trying.
Stop forcing.
Breathe.

Then shed all that you'll never be.
And hold on to all that you are.
Let it feel like the tension of an overcast sky.
Wait for the first drop of release.
Then gather the truest parts back into your
body.

And as if the high priestess herself
blessed the clouds directly overhead, let
yourself be cleansed, blessed, and reborn.

thirteen

When she feels possibility within that which
has felt impossible for so long. When the song
of her soul can be heard from the other side
of pain. When she can name every brick on
the wall she's built around her heart. When
she realizes that she's self-sabotaging. When
she can no longer shake off her dreams in the
daylight. When she knows the decision to feel
is necessary. When the promise of healing
means believing in herself. When the scariness
becomes purpose. When she understands that
her darkness is a chance for her to choose who
she wants to be and what she offers to the
world.

fourteen

There are days when she forgets who she is.

Minutes pass slowly while years race by.

Who is that person in the mirror?

Who inhabits this bag of bones?

She's still the girl who loves living,
who notices everything new.

And there's nothing she wants more
than for herself to be true . . .

Like the feeling of music.

Like a sip of hot tea.

Like the storm that changes everything.

fifteen

The change I pray for
in the world
starts with
healing
the violence
the injustice
and oppression
within
myself
and
that
means
nothing
less
than
truly
loving
and accepting
who I am.

sixteen

Grief has no expiration date. You don't just get over inexplicable loss.

You learn to cope and hope that time will create a stronger version of you.

A version that can again
and again
and again
and again
go back and console that broken-hearted you.

A version that will carefully and lovingly listen to the sounds of your sadness.

A version that will feel the depths of what you lost and had.

A version that isn't afraid of the unknown or invisible.

A version who knows that only love will survive this oceanic, otherworldly injury.

A version that has angel arms and is never, not even for a single second, afraid of feeling.

seventeen

Dad, there has always been an ocean of silence between us. A lifetime of words left unsaid. In ways I feel that I don't know you at all. I barely knew you way back then. What I now want you to know is this. I was just a child. But I knew you were broken. I don't blame you and could never hate you. I felt how the path tore at you with its jagged edges. Your unspoken pain is no stranger to my blood and bones. I carry it too. And on nights when I wonder what we would say to each other after all these years, I can't help but remember the moments before you left. For the last time. For good. You spoke to me of yourself in third person, "Your daddy loves you." And I believed you as I fell backward into a silence, without which I would never have been able to break free.

eighteen

Your darkness will come,
and when it does,
let it hold you.
Let it whisper in your ear
a story of gut-wrenching love
of heartbreak
of snowstorms and drought
of what can't be understood.
And know
it will sometimes feel like pain,
but it doesn't mean to hurt you
because it knows you've suffered enough.

nineteen

You should never have to . . .

beg someone to love you
force anyone to see you
or fight to make them stay.

Not even blood.
Not even bone.

twenty

It was hard growing up
with my mother and father long gone
some cousins liked me
some aunties felt sorry for me
and some uncles thought I was a burden.
But most preferred unwanted children
to be silent and invisible.
This is where I learned the art of shrinking
of being a wallflower
of playing small
and voiceless.
You see, when they said
Unwanted my young ears heard Unlovable
and Unworthy
and Nothing.
I am nothing.
I am nothing to them.
And nothing to you.
And nothing to anyone.
It was later in life that I realized I had to
become something to myself in order to save
my own life.

twenty-one

Stepmother, I realize now that my pain was
no match for yours. You gave my father the
ultimatum that put an ocean between him
and I, the one where you said, "It's either her
or me." He chose you. And left. And when I
surrendered to the hole in my chest, there was
something soothing in knowing that, if nothing
more, I'd be a ghost haunting both of your
pasts.

twenty-two

Even as I stand knee-deep in sadness and
emotional pain, in what feels like scary times
of this and that, my eyes still water with love,
and my heart swells with gratitude.

I shed my old skin and I hold on.
I hold on.
I hold on.

twenty-three

Like the spider,
a web I'll spin.

Like the blackbird,
I'll sing again.

Like everything matters.

~Hope

twenty-four

I don't know any woman who hasn't been to hell and back trying to find comfort in her skin. Who hasn't obsessed over weight, exercise, food, or looks. Who hasn't at least once in her life hid her menstruation, curves, sexiness, or beauty. Who hasn't felt obligated to please another. Who hasn't shrunk her intuition or intelligence. Who hasn't been objectified or silenced. Who hasn't held herself back. Who hasn't tried to erase life's inner or outer scars from her vessel. Who hasn't been judged for her years on this planet or for how good she looks. And I don't know any woman who just gets over this. Because, for a woman, it's hard to ignore the power and magnitude her body has—that she has. Because her story is every woman's story. And despite it all, I don't know any woman who isn't worthy of her strength, courage, and imagination. Who isn't capable of being the high and holy, healing damage control the world aches for right now, by empowering herself.

twenty-five

Remember:
People are the way they are because of them.
People love the way they love because of them.
People do the things they do because of them.
Not because of you.

twenty-six

She's drawn to those who know struggle as well as she does. Those who often sit in the dark with eyes closed, heart open. Those who don't respond with, "Yeah, but . . . " Those who understand beyond talking. A silent kind of compassion. The understanding she needs on days when the light just isn't there.

twenty-seven

If the way they "do"
or the way they "love"
hurts you,
belittles you,
or if they use guilt
or abuse
to make you stay,
then you get to choose to accept it or not.

You don't owe it to anyone
"to stay"
especially if it hurts.

twenty-eight

Sit in the darkness if you want to feel better.
'Cause there is no other way out of this mess.
Be still and feel until you can't tell where you
begin and shadow ends. It will scare you with
depth and spook you with glory. Let it show
you a new way, and a stronger, softer, more
magical you.

twenty-nine

She learns, grows, and becomes so strong and
so brilliant as much through suffering as
triumph, as much through screaming her head
off in the dark as sitting quietly among swaying
flowers, as much through losing every single
thing as receiving the lot of her wildest dream.

thirty

She forgets
that even without a single human to turn to
she's still
a daughter
of Earth
and she can always
always
turn to Her.

thirty-one

All that she endured is not in vain.
Because the gift of giving is within the pain.

The consciousness of the world
births the healing it needs.
And it will repeat and repeat,
until Earth meets her knees.

She was born an angel,
and that painful story she holds,
is one of warriorship,
where healing unfolds.

She often visits the baby she was in the womb,
to let her know
that not all is gloom and doom.

That she's just as important
as the oldest trees and the sky above,
that she may rest assured,
life is a mission of Love.

thirty-two

The feelings of not believing I could change
have made me unconsciously

run
hide
self-destruct
binge
deprive
hate
rage
and cry.

It was only when I became ready to heal that I
realized I had been

running
hiding
self-destructing
bingeing
depriving
hating
raging
and crying.

thirty-three

No one told me it would be like this. The sharp edges. The blindfolds. The hurt people hurting people. No one told me it could hurt like this. The deaths. The betrayals. The loneliness. No one told me about all the unnecessary suffering. The time. The fear. The scarcity. No one told me how to pick up the pieces. The disconnectedness. The silence. The waiting. No one told me how people change. The lies. The projection. The misunderstandings. They tell you it's easier to be mad, cold, and void. They show you how to numb yourself and to look away. They pretend your actions don't matter, that you're stuck no matter what, so don't waste your energy trying. There's something else they never told me: that I, like the lotus, can grow wildly out of the heaviest muck, that my pain has purpose, and that my struggle is my relentless, soulful sparkle.

thirty-four

To let time create distance between you and the moment when pain's arrows pierced your heart can be the hardest thing. But you've got to let go. Do it now. You've done all you could do. You lit all the lanterns that would light. Let time take your hand and guide you forward. Keep standing up for your true self and trust that your authentic vibration will let the world know where you are and how to find you.

thirty-five

It took being betrayed to realize how she's been betraying herself.

It took failing to understand the hurtful actions of others to realize how her own pain is misunderstood.

It took seeing those she loves fight to stay behind their veil of delusion to find the courage to peek behind her own.

It took acknowledging the brokenness of the world to dare making herself whole.

thirty-six

I went back to the newborn baby who felt
afraid. I went back to the child who wanted to
feel safe. I went back to the teenager who
longed to be heard. I went back to the young
woman who craved love. I went back to the
adult who prayed for direction. I went back to
the human being who blamed herself. For
being abandoned, rejected, and left behind.
And I saw how unworthy she thought she was
of safety and affection. How unwanted she felt.
How alone she seemed. How she suffered in
silence for so long . . . I looked into tear-filled
eyes and gathered the newborn, the child, the
teenager, the young woman, the adult, and the
human being I am and had been into my arms,
and with a love I knew was mine, I carried us
all to the other side of pain.

thirty-seven

Love the stale glitter on your tired face
and the tangled bird's nest you call hair.

Love your wobbly messiness, bad grammar,
and sailor-cussing flair.

Love the crystals falling out of your bra
and the feathers stuffed in your pocket.

Love the scariness of what you know is held
in your little heart locket.

thirty-eight

Find the warrior within and listen to what she says:

I am free. I am cosmic. I can change.
I am beautiful.
I am calm. I am grounded. I am worthy.
I am ecstatic. I am capable. I am confident.
I can follow through.

I am electric and empowered.
I am a winner.
I am messy and imperfect.
I can make nourishing decisions.
I am not my parents or my society.

I am an alchemist, creator, and magic-maker.

I am love.
I am a sparkle in the dark.
I am life.
I am me and it is enough.

thirty-nine

Sit long in Nature, and after a while, she'll sit within you. Let her take away your name, your history, and everything on your to-do list. Let her mess up your hair, dirty your feet, and awaken you to your inner mermaid.

forty

She spits storms
and grows flowers on her tongue.

She is the frigid, sharp edges
of the crescent moon,
and the steamy lapping
of a raging June.

She is the queen
who crowns the trees.
She's the breath of a wild galaxy
disguised as summer's breeze.

forty-one

Those who find her crazy
are too sane for the magic of the stars,
the wisdom of the trees,
and the power of her howl on a full moon eve.

forty-two

Sometimes she's the lone wolf girl.
Sometimes she's the chaotic beehive queen.
Sometimes she's the open ocean mother.
Sometimes she's the rain-soaked forest sister.
Sometimes she's the sturdy mountain midwife.

And sometimes,
she's the wild flower fairy
basking in the moonlight.

forty-three

It's a path of remembering. It's an unfiltered pull toward something soft. It's a blend of water, fire, wolf, and moth.

It's something clear and mysterious. It's the song of your soul. It's a rhythm of pieces, a feeling of whole.

It's an invitation and vibrant dance of imagination, beauty, knowing glances.

It's not always easy and rarely smooth. It's light and dark, sun and moon. It's the shape of a woman's body. It's aliveness calling you.

Can you hear it?

forty-four

Forget
all of your goals,
except
the one to heal.

forty-five

She's sensitive and vulnerable,
thoughtful and brave.

She's present and future,
battle and play.

She's child and tiger,
chaos and right.

She's seeker and leader,
bliss and night.

forty-six

To me, being spiritual means:

Whispering to trees,
laughing with flowers,
falling in love with sunsets,
consulting the water,
and worshipping the stars.

One hand to my heart.
One hand to Earth.
And sparkles.
Tons of them.

forty-seven

She is a real person. She struggles, and she
sparkles. She is no longer afraid to say what
makes her angry, sad, or what she thinks is
unfair. She's not afraid to admit that at times
she feels worthless, lost, or not enough. She's
refusing to hide from love, beauty, aliveness,
magic, and abundance. She won't edit the sad
or messed up parts of her story, or the holy
magnitude of her triumphs, to make anyone
comfortable. She is a real person. She
struggles, and she sparkles. She is a real
person.

~Disclaimer

forty-eight

When I tell a woman she's beautiful,
it has nothing to do with her looks,
but everything to do with
how she walks through the fire,
burns her masks,
and stands naked,
draped in her soul.

forty-nine

The only way to break the spell on my
wounded world is to say yes to the fire in my
heart. Because my self-limiting beliefs are a
mere pile of tinder, shame the spark, and fear
the oxygen it takes to burn it all to ashes. The
wall between me feeling stuck and my dream
life is thinner than I think, and it doesn't
take a giant leap to get there, but a gentle
adjustment of perspective, a small step in the
other direction, and a soft lean into that big,
warm "yes."

fifty

She acts tough,
but every night prays
for trees and wildflowers.

She acts tough,
but love and caring
are her best superpowers.

fifty-one

The nourishment of pain is yours.
Weave its magic into your life.
Let it cloak your shoulders.
Let it open you like a flower.
Let it educate your heart
and reveal your superpower.

fifty-two

The rules of this game are yours.
The arena is yours.
The sweat, fire, and burn are yours.
The triumphs are yours.
And like everything in Life,
it is all waiting for you.

fifty-three

There's a time for cord-cutting, letting go, and breaking free.

There's a time for shape-shifting, evolving, and time-traveling.

There's a time for forgiveness, stillness, and empathy.

There's a time for heart-mending, strength-building, and surviving.

There's a time for waking wild, moon-bathing, and being messy.

There's a time for just letting you be you and what will be, be.

fifty-four

I had a dream last night that I was visiting Earth. I heard myself say, "I've missed this place," as I gazed off into the distant trees.

The forest smelled like my favorite childhood pillow, and it felt like summer under a pale blue sky.

When I woke up, I couldn't help but wonder, "Where have I gone? Who have I been? Am I an alien, an immigrant on Earth? A cosmic traveler?"

And then I remembered that we're flying, indefinitely, through time and space, and somehow that felt soothing, because there's so much knowing in all that unknown.

fifty-five

I choose to fully inhabit my body, to slay my inner demons, and to nurture my inner child.

I choose to go the distance to live my dreams, not just to survive, but to thrive. I choose to walk my own path. I choose to settle only for what I want. I choose to write to understand myself, not to be understood. I choose to share my story, not to be heard, but to hear the echo of my truth. I choose to be me no matter how strange, weird, or uncomfortable it may be for others. I choose to let go of the people who make me feel insignificant. I choose to free my past. I choose to forgive, because it's freeing for me. I choose to stop fighting life, because life knows that I'm already strong.

fifty-six

Don't waste your time on anyone or anything that makes you feel less like yourself. I've found that one of the worst feelings in the world is waking up to my soul whispering: "Stop being an imposter, this isn't you."

So I return to the trees, and that is where I see my reflection and feel the scratchiness on my shoulder blades as I grow back my wings.

I let go of who I was to dare and discover who I am in the freedom of this moment, and just like the wind, I know I'll change again, but gasp with excitement at the mere thought of soaring in the breath of now.

~RIP Old Self, You Served a Great Purpose

fifty-seven

She wants to know what love is, how colors are made, where dreams live. She wants to know why the world is a mess, why change is hard, if angels exist. (She thinks they do.) She wants to know the formula for peace and what it feels like to sleep alone in a forest. She wants to know how animals communicate. She wants to know the point of hope, the source of compassion, and how Earth spins. She wants to know the chemistry of moonlight, the mechanics of fear, and what happens after death. She wants to know what it means to be pure, whole, everything, and nothing. She wants to know about past lives. She wants to know where we come from, how storms are born, and what freedom is. She wants to know if personal growth comes from becoming or being. She wants to know how much room courage leaves for fear. She wants to know the blueprint of miracles, who listens to our prayers, and what it feels like to forgive. She wants to know what love is, how colors are made, and where dreams live.

fifty-eight

When you realize you've felt like a caged animal for too long, but suddenly hear the click of the lock in the door to freedom . . .

When you discover that the lock was never a lock, but a locket in the shape of your heart carrying the beat to the anthem of your soul . . .

When it turns out that the walls keeping you safe, the ones echoing the sounds of your own drum, were mere illusions of your overly protective mind . . .

When you hear the sound of the universe, not outside of you, but within you, as you . . .

And you step both feet outside of the walls and into a new kind of freedom, a different kind of you.

And you roar with an aliveness that breaks through illusion, that breaks through you into You.

fifty-nine

She wanted to be known
as the kind of feminist
who gave humanity
back her crown.

sixty

When she learns
to hold her own hand,
she befriends
the entire world.

sixty-one

I accept who I am today
and forgive who I was.
I did the best I ever could.
I am new now.

~Daily Mantra

sixty-two

At a point in her life, it felt like the people in her life came and went like seasons. She realized she was growing and that it was natural to see friends, lovers, places, and things come and go. As she evolved, so did her interests and priorities. Some were creatively inspired by her growth. Some judged her, unready to experience their own personal change. But she had a soulful mission. So she surrounded herself with women who had their own intentions and goals, but more than anything, women who wanted to heal themselves and who also wanted to see her heal, rise, and manifest her dreams.

sixty-three

She's made a vow to the power that rules her
magical fate. She's dancing with Kali at her
dragon's weathered gate.

She need not fear or ever feel abandoned, for
she speaks to trees, her world enchanted.

The song of her flute is graceful, at ease:
May we all surrender. May we all live free.

She sees the good in you and the good in me.
She climbs her dream ladder to divinity.

She's the light on your path, the one who
remembers that everything is awaiting your
rise from the embers.

sixty-four

Stop trying to be less of yourself. Be too
powerful, too loving, too whole, too magical.
Be too sparkly.

~To the Reader

sixty-five

Sometimes I have to remind myself:

No one's love is more important than my own,
and I don't need anyone to tell me "good job"
or "you're on the right track." External
validation, permission seeking, and approval are
things of my wounded past. My precious
heart is strong and clairvoyant, and the link
between this human experience and the
transmission prescription of archangels. Every
breath dreams me more and more awake. I am
me and it is enough.

sixty-six

She knows that she'll get her butt kicked if she
chooses aliveness. Her light will blind others.
Her darkness will not let her fit in. Her success
will provoke conflict. Her ways of healing will
be judged. Her enemies will want her to
cower. And fear will do its best to take her
down. So she draws a circle around herself and
keeps opening up. Because aliveness is
freedom. She's embracing the risk to bypass the
ordinary. And she is exactly what the
world needs right now.

sixty-seven

Exhale deeply and completely.
Because you are already beautiful.
Because you are already enough.

Inhale fully.
Because you are already powerful.
Because you are already genius.

Exhale deeply and completely.
Because you are already blazing.
Because you are already heaven.

Inhale fully.
Because you are already holy.
Because you are already magic.

~Breathe

sixty-eight

Dance in the forest alone with the trees. Paint your face as wicked as you please. Dress to shine the magic of your body. Reclaim your home as one holy hobby.

sixty-nine

Give up all the worlds, places, relationships, jobs, diets, programs, and things you've been trying to force yourself into. You were born to be free. Like falling leaves, the hummingbird, lioness, and honeybee. You're a land-loving mermaid, a dreamer among trees. You are the gatherer, the storyteller, part of an invisible mystery . . .

and visible proof of magic.

seventy

She's a wild, little bouquet. It's taken time, but she's learned that even while standing knee-deep in pain, she doesn't have to project it. No matter how lonely or cold her inner fortress becomes, there are always other ways. So instead of dishing out her hurt, she softens her hands and offers touches of love. And that's what makes her so courageous. And epic.

seventy-one

A part of her is gone.
She felt like summer and deep water.
But came dressed as a hurricane.
She's the one she's going to miss the most.
The one she misses already.
The wild girl with stars in her eyes
and storm in her hair.
She was somatic and moony.
And before she left, she whispered:
"Stop being a victim of your beautiful life."

seventy-two

Your pain will transform you.
Your story will enliven the world.
Your truths will magnetize your tribe.
Your weird will set you free.
You are worthy.
You are worthy.
You are worthy.

seventy-three

She's learning
to love herself
like the love of her life.

seventy-four

The wisdom I gained from realizing that it was easy for people in my life to let go of me was that I didn't have to abandon myself.

seventy-five

Miracles
don't happen
by chance.
They happen
when you step
into the flames
that burn your soul.

seventy-six

She wasn't angry.
She was broken.

She wasn't sad.
She was torn open.

She wasn't impatient.
She was ablaze.

She wasn't mad.
She was wild and brave.

seventy-seven

Bringing light to your darkness is nothing
compared to deciding what you're going to do
with all that power.

seventy-eight

Lose your fear.
Be brave with your words.
Give thanks and take only what you need.
Express yourself honestly with your body.
And visit your tree.
Start by looking into the mirror.
And tenderly accept what you see.

seventy-nine

You are the incubator
the reservoir
and the chalice well.

You are the dream-maker
the time-traveler
and the sign that reads "this way."

You are the wild field of flowers
the rebellious lightning bolt
and the rich, fertile soil.

And it doesn't matter if you are
urban or country
frontline or back row
high-strung or easy-does-it.

You are the magic walking middle-earth.
And you don't have to give a fine damn about
fitting in anymore.

eighty

Tonight I write the manifesto of my soul, the angel guiding me from unconscious to whole. Setting free the me that no longer exists, to the song of heart I resist yet persists. It's taken decades to heal what I thought was a burden. This gift I now befriend found behind a dark curtain. To the power of my pain, and the rebirthed me, I call the North, Jai Ma! Blessed Be! To my smoldering ashes and my heavy crown, one hand on my heart, one hand on the ground. To facing fear and honoring death, to life, to spirit, to creation, and to breath.

eighty-one

She traded in
her need for approval
for the heaviness
of her crown.

eighty-two

Because sometimes to survive
twenty-one years
thirty-one years
forty-one years
fifty-one years
you've got to find the courage
to lay your heart down
and dance wildly around it
with all you've got
without a care in the world
and know
that the warm blood in your body
the sweat on your skin
and the tears in your eyes
is the journey of
feeling
healing
and revealing.

eighty-three

When you share a sunrise
that awakens your thousand-year-old soul.

When he calls it a rainbow
and you feel connected.

When the preciousness of the moment
consumes every cell.

And you know one lifetime isn't enough
to taste the fullness of love.

~A Morning with Albert

eighty-four

May you remember your ability to choose
what is deeply nourishing. May you ignite your
power to make choices that align with your
soul. May you take action in the name of your
authentic fire. May you find the courage to
heal, be free, and grow.

~New Moon Blessing

eighty-five

When she shifted from competition to
collaboration, all the women around her
became radiant stars in a dark blue sky, each
one striking and rising, without trying to
outshine.

eighty-six

Just like
the raging wind
the erupting volcano
the forest fire
and the rainstorm,
no one can tell
the awakening queens
the warrior women
and the earth angels
to calm down.

eighty-seven

Come at me with your most dangerous storm, and watch me explode into a million unsullied rainbows.

Bite me as hard as you can to crush my bones with your muck-covered lies, and watch me transform into a continent of untouched forest.

Inject me with your deepest fear, and watch me walk fearless and naked through the fires of hell, a flame-resistant angel of Earth with my wings at full breadth and a smile across my face.

My power is no longer a well for you to sip from.

My worth is no longer yours to take.

eighty-eight

May you
find power in your sensitivity,
art in your vulnerability,
sparkle in your suffering,
imagination in your imperfections,
and un-shame your pain into soulful purpose.

~Eat My Stardust

eighty-nine

I have a scar.
I have an epic story.

ninety

Pain has led me through decades of self-sabotage and playing small. It made me apologetic for the space I took up, embarrassed by the sounds of my howls and insecure about the creativity that bled from my claws. For as long as I remember, I didn't like myself despite knowing that I had something to offer. My hidden unhappiness kept me in toxic relationships, malnourished friendships, and poisonous mindsets just so I didn't have to be alone. I let people think I was weak, and I let them believe that I was someone else just to fit in. Then one day, I had enough. I began to allow myself to do the things that made me feel empowered, and I learned a new language of pain. My life started to change. I let go of underserving people, places, and things to magnetize a new tribe. None of this happened overnight. It has been a humbling lifetime process for me, but now I know that the courage to own my story of pain, to feel it and claim its power, took me out of exile and into a radiant, healing, speckled light.

ninety-one

Deep within me, courage resides. My fiercest
dream is on the verge of being born. The pain
of the world can be felt within, but this isn't the
beginning of any end. I'm finding my way
back to my body, my most heart-loyal friend.
Girl, I've got what it takes to heal this holy
place. Because you and I are the women, the
daughters of a rising grace.

ninety-two

Let everyone who taught you about all the ways to feel insignificant lead you to all that is significant about you.

ninety-three

What if sensitivity is a sign you've broken through? What if vulnerability is a symptom of your growing strength? What if feeling like you no longer fit in is the confirmation of your initiation toward soulful truth? What if fear is the way out of self-sabotage? What if confusion is the ignition of your imagination? What if restlessness is proof you have ample energy? What if resistance represents a door to unlimited possibility? What if you woke up today and weren't afraid anymore? What if all you need to do is be you? Now.

ninety-four

When you want the same safety, beauty, comfort, and protection for the world as you want for yourself, you move us all a little bit closer toward heaven on Earth.

ninety-five

I don't want to wait until the last dance to realize that when life whispered, "Take a chance," it meant for me to follow the ache in my heart, the hunger in my bones, and to allow myself to be led by the footsteps of my soul.

ninety-six

I used to think I'd be alone forever. Strange. Misunderstood. Aching to create, but too hurt to move. Then one day, I started to share my weird. My bizarre, my darkest-part-of-the-night poetry, and the scarred lining of my broken, hopeful heart. I was greeted by other wounded and open beings. Dream weavers, love warriors, and magic-makers. And together, we're walking each other home.

ninety-seven

When I realized my pain came from wanting to be liked, I started to love myself.

When I realized my pain came from wanting to be acknowledged, I began to see the woman I really was.

When I realized my pain came from hoping to be special, I set out to explore the depths of my normality.

When I realized my pain came from wanting to be held, I let myself feel the sensations of my body.

When I realized my pain came from craving to belong, I took the first steps to nourish my authentic self.

When I realized my pain originated from the actions of others, I began to accept responsibility for my own story.

When I realized my pain came from chasing those who didn't want me, I set myself free.

~The Ecstasy within the Ache

ninety-eight

She wakes you up.
She reminds you
that you can make things happen.
That you have something wicked to offer.
She cures your low self-esteem.
And watches you cry mid-story.
She shouts, "Hold on!"
Even when there's nothing left in you.
Even when the life you've built gets broken.
She knows you can keep yourself together.
She sees you.
And she bows to your risk.
'Cause queens never give up.
She wakes you up.
That's just what she does.

~Best Friend

ninety-nine

She lets go of one life, only to enter another.
Clarity dwindles and is then birthed again.
Creativity dies and returns from its ashes. Love
fades and blossoms passionately once more.
Pain loosens its grip only for her wounds to
reopen.

To truly live means to embrace and withstand
new beginnings, scary endings, and all the
meaningful stuff in between over and over
again. Whether it's mundane or magical,
heaven or hell, is up to her.

one hundred

The more I allowed myself to inhabit the space encapsulated by my skin, the closer I came to understanding that the mother, sister, and best friend I had always longed for were already within me. The home, the family, the four walls, the arms to hold me, and the eyes to see me that I forever sought were already there. Waiting to be received.

one hundred one

It may help, but the words "I'm sorry" will not heal you. The damage done isn't a weight you have to carry, and the word "victim" isn't a label you have to wear. Pain is but a torch that all heart warriors, earth angels, and wounded healers bear. Your salvation is discovering how that pain revealed a hole in your soul and a crack in humanity, and your freedom, our victorious evolution, is the courageous compassion you find for yourself so you can become whole again. Because you are the cure, and your story is the healing elixir for the poison in the world.

~Your Pain Can Set Us Free

one hundred two

The "ugly" queen between your legs is not only normal and gorgeous, but empowers, heals, and gives life to the whole world.

one hundred three

I was too broken to ever return to the person I
had been. The buildup of not being seen by
my own blood, of being told that everything
was okay when it wasn't, of being shunned,
bullied, and ignored, of facing pain with no
one to turn to or trust. I survived by acting like I
didn't care . . . about me. Like nothing bad had
really happened. Like I could just muscle
through. I wasn't saved by someone else's risk
to love me. I wasn't awakened by anyone's
confidence in my power. I was rescued by the
courage to be vulnerable. I was relieved by my
sensitivity. I was encouraged and transformed by
my own belief in me.

one hundred four

May you discover
what it truly means
to love
and accept yourself
in this lifetime.

~Full Moon Blessing

one hundred five

I asked my heart to tell me:
How to change so I could be worthy.
How to act so I could be loved.
How to look so I could be accepted.
What to say so I could be significant.
How to think so I could succeed.

And it said:
Stop trying to fit in with people, places, and
things that make you feel unworthy, unloved,
inadequate, insignificant, and stagnant.

one hundred six

A queen you have always been.
A queen you must always be.

For you're filled with your own kind of magic.

The wanderer
creator
lover
mother
dreamer
between Earth and sky.

The world is about to change.
And that is why you are here.
This is a new beginning of your life.

A queen you have always been.
A queen you must always be.

one hundred seven

There's a changing of the guards happening
right now inside of you. Peace has found her
way. Grace and her cavalry are here to stay.
There are archangels on your side. Waiting
for your sign. You can no longer deny it. If
you don't believe me, ask your soul. And it will
whisper: "Surrender, and let my love swallow
you whole."

one hundred eight

It took me many years,
and getting over myself,
and trusting,
and believing,
and giving in to the knowing,
that if I want
to be loved,
I must be love,
that if I want
to be beautiful,
I must choose
to nourish myself
beautifully,
that if I want
to be free,
I must forgive
because I don't deserve
to remain on any hook
when my wings
belong in the sky.

one hundred nine

When you care for someone.
Catch yourself.

When you know their story.
Catch yourself.

When you know you can't hold space.
Catch yourself.

When they start to share what's hurting their
heart.

Catch yourself.
So you don't impatiently respond,
unintentionally judge, or use their wounds
against them.

Catch yourself.
So you don't project your own pain, assign
shame, or unintentionally add a layer of blame.

Catch yourself.
And use this as a moment to practice a sun and
moon kind of love.

Catch yourself.
And just say:
"I believe you."

one hundred ten

Emotional pain
you don't know
how it
affects you
'til you do
then you get
to choose how
to empower
that wound.

one hundred eleven

Woman,
why do you have to be so hard
when you're strongest when you're soft?

one hundred twelve

I used to try to be Good. I thought no one
wanted me as I was, so Good was my go-to.
But Good got me nowhere. Not like Truth.
Truth, she tore me to shreds, devoured me
whole, and spit me out shaking and new. Truth
carries a box of matches in her pocket. While
Good, she's afraid of fire. Truth keeps me
real, even if it makes everyone in the room
uncomfortable. Truth, unlike Good, doesn't let
me bow down to undeserving soapboxes. Truth
doesn't let me give in to bullies, misguided
and fear-based criticism, or cowards. Truth
is a queen and a humanitarian, while Good,
she's a silent, scared little sheep. Truth knows
that Good dulls my already radiant, fierce, and
loving soul. Good showed me how to hide my
wings, my sharp teeth, and angel vision. Truth
taught me to be brave. Truth taught me how to
respect myself. Truth, my friend, allows me to
hold impenetrable space for any story, but first
and foremost, my own. And Truth, well, she
changes everything, and, friend, she's coming
for you.

one hundred thirteen

Welcome to your personal apocalypse. If you're feeling torn apart, if you're on the bloodiest battlefield of your life, if you're writing the eulogy for the person you used to be, if all the rigid habits you've been holding on to are slipping through your fingers, if you're over being excessive, exhausted, and over-productive, if your soul won't leave you alone, if you're done hiding, if you're literally sick and tired of your own excuses, if all the plates you're carrying are falling to the floor, if truth has you and will not let go, if your personal freedom, emotional literacy, and authenticity feel dangerous, if you've finally realized that there's no separation, that there's absolutely no distance or difference between the mess you are right now and your absolute dream self, welcome. You're not alone.

one hundred fourteen

To be blessed by everything you hate, to shift
from suffering to ecstasy of ache. This is your
year to no longer be who you were, to rise
from the embers, to be guided by Her. This
is your year to be carried by grace, out of the
matrix and away from the race. This is your
year to be the clear-visioned goddess, to bear
the heaviness of a crown, a sacred promise.
This is your year to live the life of your dreams,
to heal, to witness, to be the one who queens.
This is your year to forever change the rest, to
un-tame, to shift, to lead, and to live blessed.

~Woman, This Is Your Year

why i love stardusted women

aquarius woman

She soars to the rhythm of her own
eccentricity. She thrives on being herself. She's
mysterious yet relatable. She's a believer yet
detached. She's an introverted extrovert. She's
the mesmerizing song of the uncaged bird.
She's a chic old soul. A freethinker and
liberated lover. She's unconventional and
never needy. She cuts strings of conformity
and drowns mediocrity. She leads the way by
being her own inner freedom fighter. A life-
breathing tempest. An independent enigma.
She's the four-winded queen, an endangered
species, an optimistic visionary, and the
courageous authenticity the world needs.

pisces woman

A free-spirited enchantress, artist of life, and
keen observer. She dreams effortlessly in the
daylight. She's a playful muse and a loving
wonderer. She sprinkles magic everywhere, as
if it were the most natural thing in the world.
She's the rain patiently waiting within the
clouds. She's the dreamy mist covering the
mountains. She's the beauty of morning dew
and the depth of Mother Ocean. She carries
with her ancient secrets and the mystery of the
flowing river. She's gentle and exciting. She's
sensual and unpredictable. She's curious even
while sitting still. She's got the spirit of a fairy,
the wisdom of Earth's womb, and the ability to
awaken your inner mermaid. She's sexy, easy
to love, and an old soul. She's the kind of
treasure you hope to find and keep for life. Her
heart medicine will make you feel like it's safe
to be yourself. She's the definition of cozy.
There's nothing weak about this woman. Her
heart is a roar and she won't look away from
love. This extraordinary, empathetic queen
makes you, me, and the world feel courageous
and whole.

aries woman

An independent Wonder Woman. She's a fire-breathing feminine creature. A kick-starter. A siren. An inner freedom fighter. The first note of the battle song. She's the one you want on the frontline of life. Her torch is relentlessly ablaze. She's fiery and impatient. She's fierce and childlike. She's exciting and unpredictable. She's both whole heart and soul and not afraid to draw blood. She can't be imitated or duplicated, and can take any amount of criticism. She sips the magic of dawn and her energy lasts until long after dusk. She's intelligent and unstoppable. All her gears are set to an optimistic forward focus. A majestic force, her magic will lift you up and reignite the fire of your heart's mission and soul's cause. Her natural, playful nature accepts any challenge. She's a fearless warrioress and a magnetic, inspiring queen who walks her talk.

taurus woman

She's the kind of nectar that can't be messed with. She's tender, caring, and superstrong. A wildflower that survives the frost and the storm. She's accountable for herself and slow to anger. With legendary stamina, she can handle a lot but knows her limits. A gentle force that can't be pushed over, she's content with who she is and doesn't waste time on worrying about how others shine. There's no sweating the small stuff. She holds her own. She's an original earth mama. Her energy is grounded and her presence soothing. She inspires all to act, not just talk. She's a quality over quantity kind of gal. Stable and dependable, she won't settle for anything less than what she loves. Her goddess power is showing others their strength and resilience. This queen makes you feel safe. Her magic will ground you, and she'll never ever doubt your dreams.

gemini woman

She embodies every bit of what it means to be a woman. She's confident and sees no reason not to speak her mind. Like a breath of fresh air, she's unpredictable and spontaneous. She's adaptable and a natural pick-me-up in any situation. She's the opposite of boring and stagnant. She's clever and inquisitive. If she's in your life, your dull moments will be few. She magnetizes and enchants with her gift of wit and charm. A fast-moving cloud, you can't pin her down, let alone define her. Like the wind, she's restless and likes to move. A shape-shifting goddess with the energy of a hummingbird and the wisdom to reinvent herself effortlessly and easily with the seasons and cycles of her life. A flirty creature. A gravity-defying doer. This fun-loving, high-in-demand, lightning-fast queen is a keeper of mystery and the woman of our dreams.

cancer woman

She's calm, reflective water. Everything about her is peaceful, enchanting, and adoring. Like the ocean forever adoring and caressing the shore, she's a fierce, loyal, and exceptional lover through and through. She may sometimes come across as shy, but this gal is warm-blooded and even more so, mysterious, sexy, and cool. She's rarely chatty. She knows how to hold space for you. This goddess makes the happiness of those she loves a priority. Her gift to all is tranquil wisdom and patience beyond her years. She has a wonderful, keen sense of humor. To her, water is baptismal, a blessing, and her way to connect with Mother Earth. Her crown is jeweled with intuition, her cape woven with creativity, and her scepter rules with astounding empathy. Her heart is a sanctuary and her arms feel like home. A naturally nurturing queen, her magic is pure love.

leo woman

She roars. She purrs. She shines. She struts her stuff. She's a fire-starter and a confident queen of the jungle. Intense and sizzling, she's got both eyes focused on love. An edgy lioness, sometimes dangerous but always generous and warm. She has a natural zest in any given moment and an enthusiasm for life and for the dreams of those she loves. She's protective with courage running through her veins. She's fierce, beautiful, and unforgettable. She's equipped to light up any room and to thaw the coldest of hearts. She expresses herself brilliantly with words and isn't afraid to go first. She's an adventurous warrioress that you'd be blessed to have by your side. She's got the power of a hurricane and the sensitivity to make your heart beat a little faster.

virgo woman

She's an independent queen of discernment and of keeping it real. Orderly, reliable, and loyal, this mama is grounded to Earth and dedicated to self-improvement. She's highly intuitive and sometimes reserved. She replenishes her body, mind, and soul in Nature. She's way stronger than she lets on, not easily shaken, and not the kind of maiden that needs rescued. She's the heroine of her own life. She doesn't wear her heart on her sleeve and won't reveal her vulnerability to just anyone. She's patient before she dives deep into any relationship. Her inner space is mountainous and humbled. She's led by sensations rather than emotions. She's a goddess of humanity and sees the good in all. Her presence creates an instant caring atmosphere. Her wand brings perfect order to your universe. Her heart insight can help you change for the better. She's the keeper of the kind of harmony that will help get your life so organized that you'll remember your magic and your wildness.

libra woman

She's the beautiful, friendly queen of balance and fairness. She arrives with an undeniable charm revealing a natural and gentle social magnetism. She's the weaving of a spring breeze and a strong gale. She's intelligent and timeless, gentle and fierce. Her medicine offers the meaning of liberation and the lightness of being. Her wand realigns our lives with the pull of our souls. Her heart and leadership are selfless. She's not a fighter, but a diplomat for inner peace and won't let anyone go to bed angry. A creative. A romantic. A stable creatrix and a lifetime best friend. She sprinkles beauty everywhere she goes. She leads with a Zen-like humbled scepter and a love you didn't think was possible.

scorpio woman

She's the sharp end of the knife with the depth
of the deepest sea. She flows like hot lava and
can feel like a hot spring. She's magnetic and
mysterious, sexy and strong. She's a goddess of
passion. She's intense and protective. She can
be your worst enemy or most loyal friend.
Either way, her warrior way will fascinate and
leave you hungry for more. She's a girl boss
and won't tolerate BS. She's got a fierce heart
and a piercing vision. She demands that you
bring it all. A precious and intuitive gem, she's
sensitive with strong boundaries. She's
unapologetic and not for everyone, but for
those who lean in, you'll find a wolf in wolf's
clothing, a gorgeous wildling, an enchanting
lover, and an adventurous queen.

sagittarius woman

She's the wild archer with fire-breathing
arrows. She's earthbound and otherworldly.
She's paving her own brave way without trying
to be understood. No one can hold her down.
She makes the ordinary an adventure. As
restless as she is, she's got mountain-like
presence. She's awkward with grace. She'll offer
you sips of her spirit and expect nothing
in return. She'll make you laugh and isn't
afraid to cry. Her enthusiasm spreads like
creative wildfire. She's got the depth of an old
soul and the wisdom of the ocean. She always
chooses aliveness, even when it feels too much.
She is the queen of reinventing herself. She
does her best work in the dark. She's two
heaping cups of wicked stardust. She's the
conjurer of your inner beauty. She sees you.
She's not a victim. She's a warrior and a
survivor. Her authenticity is intoxicating. She
owns her messiness and is every bit beautiful.

capricorn woman

She scales mountains. A real all-weather woman. Her armor is tough, but underneath, she's sensitive, soft, and sometimes shy. Her inner circle is small and her loyalty deep. A lone wolf, but a great team player. She's ambitious. A winner on life's battlefield. She's loyal to her dreams and content on her path. Her success is fueled by wit and diligence. This gal is the perfect braiding of a practical nature with VIP sophistication. She's no-nonsense but with a sense of humor. She can't be pushed or rushed anywhere, but sets her own pace. She's often regarded as the Queen of Ice, but earn her trust, and consider yourself both blessed and lucky in love and friendship. This cool warrioress is patient, thoughtful, and nurturing, like Mother Earth. She loves to make her life and the lives around her beautiful. She makes sure that those she loves (and who love her back) are cared for, seen, and safe. And no matter how loud or quiet she chooses to be, she remains a dependable, radiant superhero of our wildest dreams.

Did any of these words touch you?

I'd love to hear from you.

Write to me:
tanya@theshebook.com

stay close

Woman, This Is Your Year—
For the Awakening Woman:

theshebook.com

I Used to Try to Be Good—
Un-shame Your Pain:

thugunicorn.com

Feel, Heal and Reveal
the Sparkle That Is You:

eatmystardust.com

May we raise the bar for how we live our lives. May we ridiculously increase the amount of peace, play, creativity, beauty, love, and joy in everything we do. May we all sip from the wisdom of our suffering. And awaken with the courage to share our stories that can heal our inner and outer worlds.

about the author

Tanya Markul is dedicated to helping others heal by holding sacred space for their stories and by unlocking the impossibility of shape-shifting their pain into soul-led healing purpose. Her medicine beckons the brave curiosity to look within, brings a sense of humor to cracked surfaces, unveils the beauty of hidden authenticity, and conjures the courage to love and accept oneself in this lifetime. She is an advocate of imagination, a creative midwife, and a rebel for reinvention and the unconventional. She empowers with words, the unseen world, sensitivity, and vulnerability.

acknowledgments

Thank you to my dear husband, my sons, and my family in Denmark. Thank you to all of my soul sisters and friends. Thank you to my community. Thank you to Tim Bjørn and the bear family. Thank you to all the challenges, teachers, lanterns, and healers that have inspired my life and broken me open.

Thank you Earth, Nature, my spirit family, angel guides, and all the helpers in the unseen world. Thank you, Life, thank you for every single breath and every single experience.

Thank you, Dearest Reader.
Thank you with all of my heart.